WORKBOOK

for

OUTLIVE

THE SCIENCE & ART OF LONGEVITY

By Brighter Health Publishing

Published by Brighter Health Publishing
ISBN: 9798862147735
Printed in the United States of America

CONTENTS

INTRODUCTION

SUMMARY

In the introduction to Outlive, Dr. Peter Attia shares a vivid dream he experienced while training to become a surgeon in an intense surgical resident program. In the dream, he was frantically trying to catch as many eggs as he could as they fell out of the sky, dropped by an anonymous man. He experienced deep sadness when he realized that there was no way he could catch every single egg.

He highlights the critical life-and-death scenario surgeons often face, especially when it comes to stubborn illnesses like pancreatic cancer. His ambition to become the best cancer surgeon often clashed with the stark reality of patients' mortality despite their efforts.

While he initially quit medicine out of frustration, he later returned with a transformative perspective, emphasizing preventive rather than reactive measures. His paradigm shift, inspired by the symbolic dream, led him to focus on preventing the causes of diseases, symbolized in his dream as the anonymous man dropping the eggs.

CHAPTER ONE
THE LONG GAME OF HEALTH AND LONGEVITY

SUMMARY

In the first chapter of Outlive, Dr. Attia touches on the idea of death, both slow and fast, as a frequent reality in his medical career. He makes it clear that this book is not about death, it's about longevity, an exploration into minimizing the 'slow death' caused by diseases and maximizing the quality of life.

Dr. Peter Attia's career shifted from performing surgeries to focusing on longevity. He discusses that longevity doesn't mean living forever or merely surviving with declining health. Instead, it implies maintaining a high quality of physical and mental health.

He notes that the slow deaths caused by 'Four Horsemen' diseases - heart disease, cancer, neurodegenerative disease, or type 2 diabetes have become prevalent due to living longer. Therefore, longevity is about understanding and confronting slow death.

Dr. Attia introduces the concept of "healthspan," emphasizing both the length and the quality of life. He highlights the need to address these chronic diseases of aging as early as possible (preferably during their inception stages) to live longer without disease.

Dr. Attia also shares his personal journey of striving for physical health necessary for emotional well-being. He reveals his ultimate aim to create an actionable guide for practicing longevity effectively, to help individuals live longer and healthier.

REFLECTION QUESTIONS FOR CHAPTER ONE

Why do you think Dr. Attia distinguishes between "fast" and "slow" deaths?

_____

_____

_____

_____

_____

How does Dr. Attia define "longevity" and "healthspan"? Why does he differentiate between lifespan and healthspan?

_____

_____

_____

_____

_____

What are the "Four Horsemen" diseases? How have these diseases impacted you personally?

_____

_____

_____

_____

_____

_____

Think about your goals surrounding longevity. Why do you want to live a happier, healthier life?

_____

_____

_____

_____

_____

_____

CHAPTER TWO
MEDICINE 3.0

SUMMARY

This section of 'Outlive' relates Dr. Attia's journey from frustration with medical training to new insights of patient care. His experience of predicting an accurate dosage timing for a septic patient eventually led to a clash with hospital hierarchy and his subsequent decision to leave medical training. This experience exposed a resistance to change and innovation, leading him to question the system.

Dr. Attia's career shift to credit risk consulting introduced a new perspective about understanding risk, which he felt was a missing link in medical training. He emphasizes the importance of understanding and managing risk, going beyond the philosophy of "do no harm," to a more nuanced approach of risk assessment.

During his break from medicine, Dr. Attia realized that his training and that of his colleagues were geared towards addressing the healthcare challenges of an earlier era – the acute illnesses and injuries handled by Medicine 2.0. These issues had shorter timelines; for cancer patients, time was a critical factor. Chronic diseases progress gradually over decades, becoming entrenched and difficult to eliminate.

This realization led him to advocate for a new perspective, Medicine 3.0, focusing on preventing ailments rather than just treating symptoms. This concept parallels the shift towards personalized medicine, yet the technology required to fully realize it is still advancing. Medicine 3.0, a radical shift in medical approach, focuses on prevention rather than treatment, considering the patient as an individual, acknowledging risk and its management, and prioritizing healthspan over lifespan.

REFLECTION QUESTIONS FOR CHAPTER TWO

How does Medicine 2.0 differ from Medicine 3.0?

_____

_____

_____

_____

_____

How does Dr. Attia's approach redefine the role of the patient in healthcare?

_____

_____

_____

_____

_____

Think about how you can honor your individuality in your healthcare journey. How can you play a more active role in the choices that define your health?

_____

_____

_____

_____

_____

_____

In order to maximize potential healthspan, one most be willing to venture outside one's comfort zone. How will you prepare yourself for these potential challenges?

_____

_____

_____

_____

_____

_____

CHAPTER THREE
OBJECTIVES, STRATEGIES AND TACTICS

SUMMARY

In the opening of this chapter, Dr. Attia tells the story of Sophie, a woman who passed away after living with pain and dementia for several years. This story of aging is a typical one- most people are spend the last few decades of their life in pain and sickness.

Dr. Attia emphasizes the importance of having objective, strategy, and tactics for a longer healthspan. Dr. Attia presents detailed accounts of his patients and their challenges to illustrate the typical decline of joy as a person ages and the consequent increase in suffering. He emphasizes the need to plan for later decades of life effectively to increase both the span and quality of life.

Our Strategy

Living longer involves delaying the onset of age-related diseases, which share age as a significant risk factor. Aging itself leaves us susceptible to ailments and affects our healthspan by weakening our internal defenses over time. To effectively address this, we must adopt a strategic approach (Medicine 3.0) rather than relying solely on tactics. Understanding the mechanisms of aging and the diseases it brings is crucial. The goal is to delay or prevent chronic diseases, achieving the long lifespans of centenarians by maintaining healthspan, which encompasses more than just being disease-free. This decline can be categorized into cognitive, physical, and emotional vectors, each needing mitigation for a healthier aging process.

The second deterioration vector concerns physical function loss, often accompanying cognitive decline but not necessarily in a set sequence. With age, muscle strength, bone density, balance, and stamina wane, impacting daily tasks and activities. The relentless progression of atherosclerosis can further hinder physical capabilities. Many people underestimate this decline's impact, and building and maintaining a foundation of fitness becomes crucial to maintaining active living.

The third vector, emotional health, is somewhat age-independent and can affect individuals early in life. Middle-aged distress can have roots in adolescence, exerting a significant influence on overall well-being. Overcoming emotional challenges is vital for physical health, happiness, and survival.

True longevity defies all vectors of decline simultaneously—cognitive, physical, and emotional. Each component is integral, and living to an advanced age without cognitive and physical vitality, or without emotional well-being, is undesirable. While death is unavoidable, the deterioration discussed here is largely preventable and optional. Proper tactics can slow or even reverse cognitive, physical, and emotional decline, as explored in upcoming chapters.

It is also important to remember that lifespan and healthspan are not independent variables. They are related to each other: increase one and you will inevitably increase the other.

Tactics

The distinction between Medicine 2.0 and Medicine 3.0 lies in the timing and integration of tactics. Medicine 2.0 responds to acute issues, while Medicine 3.0 embeds tactics into daily life. Medicine 2.0 employs procedures and medications, whereas Medicine 3.0 encompasses exercise, nutrition, sleep, emotional health, and molecules like drugs or supplements.

Exercise

The term "exercise" can encompass various activities, but the author breaks it down into essential components like strength, stability, aerobic efficiency, and peak capacity. Improving these aspects is vital for extending lifespan and healthspan. Exercise is the most potent longevity strategy, preventing cognitive and physical decline, and enhancing emotional well-being. The goal is to comprehend the reasons behind different exercises and tailor a personal fitness plan.

Nutrition

Dr. Attia avoids dictating specific diets or engaging in diet debates. Instead, he prioritizes biochemical evidence over dogma. While acknowledging the significance of what we eat, he emphasizes the importance of caloric intake as a primary factor. Achieving the right balance depends on individual factors, and the goal is to help readers discover their optimal eating pattern.

Sleep

We are just beginning to understand the importance of quality sleep when it comes to longevity. More and more research shows that it is critical for overall health.

Emotional Health

Dr. Attia admits that he has struggled his whole life with his emotional health. Emotional health is a critical factor in overall well-being and it should not be ignored. Longevity is pointless if we are not seeking to improve our emotional health.

QUESTIONS FOR CHAPTER THREE

Activity for visualizing healthspan

Using the graph below, draw your current trajectory.

Where does your line flatten out? At what point do you think you will lose your ability to do the things you love?

_____

_____

_____

_____

_____

Now draw another line on the graph–your ideal trajectory. What lifestyle changes do you think you must make in order to make that ideal trajectory a reality?

_____

_____

_____

_____

_____

Imagine being in your seventies, eighties, and nineties. What activities would you like to participate in?

_____

_____

_____

_____

_____

Reflect on your current health strategy. Is it more reactive or proactive? What positive changes would you like to try first?

_____

_____

_____

_____

_____

Think about the four tactics: Exercise, sleep, nutrition, and emotional health. Why do you think Dr. Attia focuses on these four domains?

_____

_____

_____

_____

_____

CHAPTER FOUR
CENTENARIANS

SUMMARY

The quest to uncover the secret of living longer drives our fascination with centenarians and their unique habits. Research into centenarian groups challenges the assumption that healthy behaviors are essential for extreme longevity; many centenarians smoked, drank, and had less active lifestyles. While genes play a role, studies suggest that they matter more as people age, with genes of centenarians significantly influencing their siblings' likelihood of reaching similar ages. While genetics can offer a form of luck, understanding how centenarians achieve their longevity can guide strategies to achieve similar benefits through behaviors.

Dr. Attia admits that he was initially worried that increasing longevity might lead to more decades of poor health. But these fears are challenged by a closer examination of centenarian data. While many centenarians face mortality rates and fragility, a more hopeful outlook emerges. Although they eventually succumb to diseases of aging, they tend to develop these illnesses much later in life than the general population, often decades later. Centenarians frequently defy the notion of aging as decline, as many maintain relatively good overall health, contrary to common expectations.

Despite outnumbering males by a significant margin, female centenarians often perform worse than males on cognitive and functional tests. This can be attributed to a selection process, where males who survive to 100 are generally healthier due to earlier susceptibility to heart attacks and strokes. This phenomenon creates a subset of relatively robust male centenarians. Additionally, supercentenarians and semisupercentenarians tend to be in even better health than regular centenarians, demonstrating a phase shift in their lifespan and healthspan. The goal of Medicine 3.0 is to emulate this phenomenon intentionally, aiming for a longer healthspan and shorter period of morbidity at the end of life.

Identifying longevity genes in centenarians has proven difficult due to the complex nature of genetic influence on longevity. Genome-wide association studies yielded limited results, as these individuals exhibit diverse genetic profiles. The rarity of centenarians is rooted in natural selection: evolution primarily favors genes aiding reproduction and early survival, rendering post-reproductive genetic traits less relevant. Genes linked to conditions like Alzheimer's or heart disease persist due to natural selection's diminished impact on older age health. Some of these genes might have offered advantages in earlier life stages, known as "antagonistic pleiotropy."

Several potential longevity genes have been identified, with APOE being a significant one. The

APOE gene's variants (e2, e3, e4) influence Alzheimer's disease risk and longevity. APOE e2 is associated with reduced dementia risk and higher likelihood of extreme old age. Cholesterol-related genes like CETP and APOC3 also impact longevity. Centenarians' extreme longevity is likely influenced by numerous genes, making it a cumulative effect rather than a single magic bullet, which offers hope for incremental interventions to extend lifespan and healthspan for the general population.

The genetics of extreme longevity remain a realm of uncertainty, but the potential influence of gene expression and environmental factors offers hope. Studies show that behaviors like exercise can alter gene expression towards a more youthful pattern, indicating that a combination of genetics and environment contributes to longevity, making it feasible to introduce interventions that mimic centenarians' genetic advantages.

REFLECTION QUESTIONS FOR CHAPTER FOUR

Why do you think Dr. Attia is so interested in studying centenarians?

_____

_____

_____

_____

_____

Dr. Attia mentions a "phase shift" when it comes to the healthspan of centarians. What is this phase shift?

_____

_____

_____

_____

_____

Based off what you learned in this chapter, what role do you think genetics play in longevity?

_____

_____

_____

_____

_____

_____

While we cannot alter our genome, we can alter our genetic expression. How do you think you can alter yours in a positive way?

_____

_____

_____

_____

_____

_____

CHAPTER FIVE
EAT LESS, LIVE LONGER?

SUMMARY

In the 16th century, an Italian businessman named Alvise Cornaro pioneered the practice of controlled eating for health. Overwhelmed by health issues due to excessive feasting, he adopted a Spartan diet of about twelve ounces of food daily, leading to a dramatic improvement in his health. His regimen became popular over the centuries, eventually supported by scientific experiments. The concept of caloric restriction (CR) was rigorously tested in the mid-20th century, showing that animals consuming 25-30% fewer calories while maintaining essential nutrients lived 15-45% longer, with better health. This effect, seen across various organisms, suggests that controlled hunger can enhance both lifespan and healthspan.

Dr. Attia doesn't recommend extreme caloric restriction due to practical limitations and uncertainties about its effects in complex human environments. However, caloric restriction studies have offered valuable insights into aging. These studies revealed that reducing nutrients activates pathways like AMP-activated protein kinase (AMPK), which enhances cellular stress resistance and metabolic efficiency. AMPK stimulates mitochondrial biogenesis and autophagy, a recycling process that breaks down damaged cellular components. Autophagy is vital for cellular health and declines with age, but can be triggered by interventions such as nutrient reduction, exercise, and the drug rapamycin.

Rapamycin's potential as a longevity drug goes beyond promoting autophagy, according to researcher Matt Kaeberlein. Despite its existing approvals for various uses in humans, launching a clinical trial to study its impact on aging faces challenges due to potential side effects, especially immunosuppression. Originally approved for post-organ transplant patients, the drug's immune-suppressing effects raised concerns about using it to delay aging in healthy individuals. However, a study in 2014 showed that the rapamycin analog everolimus enhanced immune responses to a vaccine in older patients, suggesting it could have immune-modulating effects rather than just immunosuppressive ones.

Previously skeptical about rapamycin's potential as a preventive therapy in healthy individuals due to its apparent immunosuppressive effects, a well-controlled study challenged this belief by demonstrating an immune-enhancing effect through cyclical administration. MTOR, composed of two complexes (mTORC1 and mTORC2), showed longevity-related benefits when mTORC1 was inhibited, achievable through brief or cyclical dosing. However, known side effects hinder clinical trials of rapamycin for delaying aging in humans. Researcher Matt Kaeberlein is conducting a large clinical trial of rapamycin in companion dogs, observing improved cardiac function, reduced inflammation, enhanced cancer surveillance, and even periodontal health through rapamycin use.

An obstacle lies in the regulatory framework rooted in Medicine 2.0, which doesn't yet fully accept "slowing aging" and "delaying disease" as legitimate endpoints. Transitioning to a Medicine 3.0 approach, where drugs maintain health rather than treat ailments, would entail greater scrutiny. The FDA's approval of the TAME trial for metformin, a diabetes drug with potential longevity benefits, suggests a shift in this direction. While measuring aging is challenging, focusing on delaying aging-related diseases as a proxy for longevity-promoting effects could lead to similar trials for rapamycin in the future.

While we still do not have one anti-aging wonder drug, we can be quite sure from these findings that **diet** and **metabolism** greatly influence longevity.

REFLECTION QUESTIONS FOR CHAPTER FIVE

Why do you think long-term calorie restriction is not a longevity solution?

_____

_____

_____

_____

_____

What is autophagy? Why is it so important for increasing longevity?

_____

_____

_____

_____

_____

Dr. Attia mentions that a transition from medicine 2.0 to medicine 3.0 will be necessary in order for longevity drugs to become FDA approved. Why do you think that is?

_____

_____

_____

_____

_____

_____

CHAPTER SIX
THE CRISIS OF ABUNDANCE

SUMMARY

America is facing an epidemic of metabolic dysfunction. Metabolism processes nutrients for energy in the body. A healthy metabolism efficiently directs nutrients to their intended destinations. Conversely, an unhealthy metabolism can lead to excess calories being stored harmfully. When consuming a doughnut, the body determines whether to convert the carbohydrate into glycogen for short-term energy. This glycogen is primarily stored in muscles and the liver, serving as a crucial energy source for activities like endurance exercises.

We possess a significant capacity to store energy as fat. Hormones, especially insulin, dictate where this energy is stored after consuming food. For active individuals, energy from food is swiftly consumed by muscles, but in a sedentary person, excess energy often accumulates as subcutaneous fat. Although subcutaneous fat is commonly viewed negatively, it serves as a safe storage site for surplus calories, maintaining metabolic health by acting as a buffer. However, excessive calorie intake beyond storage capacity leads to fat accumulation in various undesirable places within the body, including the liver, muscle tissue, and blood, resulting in negative health consequences. This harmful fat is called visceral fat.

Subcutaneous fat is thought to be relatively harmless, but visceral fat is very dangerous. Visceral fat secretes inflammatory cytokines and is linked to cancer and cardiovascular disease.

Individuals vary in their capacity to store fat. This is why some overweight people might be metabolically healthy: if they have a larger capacity to store fat, then they might have less visceral fat than someone who weighs less. This is why it is important to get a DEXA scan. A DEXA scan will help you understand how much of your fat is the dangerous visceral kind.

If fat is accumulating in undesirable places like your liver, around your heart, and particularly within your muscles, it can potentially trigger insulin resistance. Insulin resistance initiates a cascade where cells no longer respond effectively to insulin's signals, leading to high insulin levels and blood glucose levels. As this cycle continues, it elevates the risk of hyperinsulinemia, obesity, and other serious health issues, including atherosclerosis, cancer, and eventually type 2 diabetes.

Diabetes, once rare, has become a widespread epidemic, with over 11% of US adults having clinical type 2 diabetes and another 38% meeting prediabetes criteria. This rise in metabolic disease is due to a mismatch between our modern diet and our evolutionary metabolism. Our genetic makeup favored fat storage to survive times of scarcity, but in today's world of calorie abundance, this genetic trait becomes problematic. The consumption of excess fructose, a form of sugar found in fruits, contributes to metabolic dysfunction, leading to the accumulation of uric acid and associated health issues like gout and elevated blood pressure.

Fructose from whole fruits doesn't pose problems due to its slow absorption with fiber and water, but excess liquid fructose, as found in fruit juices and sugary beverages, can lead to metabolic issues. High uric acid levels from fructose consumption can indicate metabolic health problems. Fructose metabolism differs from glucose, causing rapid drops in cellular energy levels, fooling the body into thinking it needs more food and encouraging fat storage. The overwhelming consumption of liquid fructose, overwhelming the gut's capacity, leads to fat accumulation, contributing to metabolic dysfunction.

Insulin resistance is the canary in the coal mine for many diseases. It dramatically increases the risk of cancer, Alzheimer's and cardiovascular disease. The good news is that insulin resistance can be reversed through diet and exercise and sleep habits.

REFLECTION QUESTIONS FOR CHAPTER SIX

What is the crisis of abundance? How is it affecting America's health?

_____

_____

_____

_____

_____

Take a moment to assess your own health. Do you have any of the risk factors associated with metabolic syndrome? (Obesity, high BMI, etc.)

_____

_____

_____

_____

_____

Even if you are not overweight, you might be suffering from insulin resistance. What steps will you take to evaluate your metabolic health?

_____

_____

_____

_____

_____

Do you consume a high amount of fructose? (Think about fruit juice, smoothies, sodas, desserts, etc.) Write down a plan to limit your fructose consumption here:

_____

_____

_____

_____

_____

CHAPTER SEVEN
THE TICKER

SUMMARY

In medical school, Dr. Attia's pathology professor highlighted that sudden death is the most common presentation of heart disease. Despite decreased mortality from surprise heart attacks due to medical advancements, they remain fatal about a third of the time. Globally, atherosclerotic cardiovascular disease, combining heart disease and stroke, is the leading cause of death, taking 2,300 lives daily in the US alone, according to the CDC.

Heart disease and stroke, together termed atherosclerotic cardiovascular disease (ASCVD), account for the highest number of daily deaths globally, causing about 2,300 fatalities per day in the US alone, surpassing cancer. Although mortality rates have decreased for surprise heart attacks, they still result in roughly one-third of deaths. Despite having a low calcium score of 6, indicating advanced atherosclerosis, the author recognized their risk due to being overweight and insulin resistant. Atherosclerosis, while challenging, is more preventable than cancer or Alzheimer's, yet it remains the leading cause of death. Treating and preventing it early is crucial, as current guidelines have limitations in understanding and addressing the disease's progression.

Modern medicine says that thirty year old's have no business being worried about cardiovascular disease. But Dr. Attia begs to differ. He points out the blindspots that Medicine 2.0 has when it comes to cardiovascular disease. The process of atherosclerosis unfolds slowly over decades, as evidenced by lesions in younger people without major events. Most adults have vascular damage due to atherosclerosis throughout life. Despite this, interventions are often considered unnecessary if the ten-year risk of an adverse event is below 5 percent. However, thinking in terms of a lifetime horizon reveals that virtually no one is at low risk, even if the ten-year risk seems low by current standards. Earlier interventions are the key to tackling cardiovascular disease.

REFLECTION QUESTIONS FOR CHAPTER SEVEN

Activity: gain insight into your cardiovascular risk

Family History

Does your family have a history of cardiovascular issues? Make a list of anyone in your family who has heart disease or who died suddenly at a young age.

_____

_____

_____

_____

_____

Make a plan for early prevention. This can include talking to your doctor and getting blood panel tests for apoB and Lp(a). Write this plan here:

_____

_____

_____

_____

_____

Think about lifestyle factors that might be contributing to your risk of heart disease, including poor diet and smoking. List them here along with your goals on how to improve.

_____

_____

_____

_____

_____

CHAPTER EIGHT
THE RUNAWAY CELL

SUMMARY

Cancer's deadly nature stems from our limited understanding of its origins and spread. Cancer cells differ from normal cells in their uncontrolled growth, often due to genetic mutations in tumor suppressor genes like PTEN. Additionally, cancer's ability to metastasize, spreading from one part of the body to another, turns it into a systemic and fatal disease. Despite these commonalities, cancer's complexity hinders the development of a straightforward cure. The Cancer Genome Atlas, a large-scale effort to sequence cancer tumor cells, initially revealed immense genetic complexity rather than clear patterns of causation.

Cancer's true danger lies in metastasis, where cancer cells spread to other organs and become responsible for most cancer deaths. Preventing, detecting, and treating metastatic cancers is essential for significant reductions in cancer mortality. Solid organ tumors, like breast and prostate cancers, typically become lethal only when they metastasize to critical organs like the brain, lungs, liver, and bones. However, the causes of cancer metastasis remain largely unknown due to limited research funding (only 5-8% for metastasis studies) and poor detection capabilities. Despite advancements in treating metastatic cancer, systemic treatment is much more challenging than localized approaches.

Chemotherapy, while effective at killing cancer cells, lacks specificity and harms normal cells, leading to severe side effects. Modern successful treatments need to be systemic and cancer-specific. Key hallmarks of cancer identified by researchers include altered metabolism and the evasion of the immune system. Some cancer cells have unique weaknesses, like altered glucose consumption and immune evasion, which researchers are exploring as potential targets for treatment. Metabolism and immune surveillance approaches offer systemic and potentially more specific methods to combat metastatic cancers, building on decades of research in these areas.

Cancer Metabolism

Even since the discovery of the double helix shape of DNA, most cancer research has focused on the genetic components of cancer cells rather than their metabolic components. But these metabolic factors are becoming harder and harder to ignore due to the link between cancer and metabolic dysfunction.

Obesity and type 2 diabetes have emerged as significant risk factors for various cancers due to their association with inflammation and growth factors like insulin. Approximately 12-13% of global cancer cases are linked to obesity. Thirteen types of cancer, including pancreatic, esophageal, renal, ovarian, breast cancers, and more, are strongly associated with obesity. Type 2 diabetes also doubles the risk of certain cancers. Obesity-driven inflammation and insulin resistance contribute to the creation of a cancer-promoting environment. Researchers like Lew Cantley discovered that the PI3-kinase enzyme family, particularly PI3K, fuels cancer growth by enhancing glucose uptake and is activated by insulin and IGF-1, ultimately enabling cancer cell proliferation.

All of these findings suggest that metabolic therapies, including dietary changes to lower insulin levels, could potentially slow cancer growth and reduce risk. Caloric restriction in laboratory animals has been shown to decrease cancer rates. Humans on caloric restriction display lowered PI3K-associated pathways, linked to reduced insulin, although this effect occurs in non-cancer-susceptible tissues like muscle. While genetic mutations leading to cancer are hard to prevent, addressing metabolic factors is more feasible. Though cancer cells can acquire energy despite diet changes, avoiding insulin resistance and type 2 diabetes is crucial for lowering cancer risk. Achieving metabolic health is a significant aspect of cancer prevention.

Immunotherapy

Currently, immunotherapy is only effective against a small percentage of cancers. But Dr. Attia has hope that new breakthroughs are just around the corner. Combining immunotherapy with other treatments seems to be a promising new therapy. Around 80 percent of epithelial cancers contain genetic mutations that the immune system could theoretically recognize and fight. Thanks to the hard work and determination of a few scientists, immunotherapy has started to make a huge difference in the war on cancer.

Early Detection

The final weapon in our battle against cancer is early and aggressive screening. Cancer that is caught early on, while it is still in the first stages, is much easier to treat. The presence of fewer and less mutated cells means that our cancer killing weapons have a much higher chance of eradication. Unfortunately, Medicine 2.0 is focused on screening patients only when they are a certain age or if they are high risk. Dr. Attia uses the example of colon cancer to illustrate his point that screening should be conducted on a much broader level. Colon cancer screenings are usually reserved for patients 50 and older. But colon cancer is relatively easy to detect and Dr. Attia recommends that patients be screened at the age of 40.

According to Dr. Attia, cancer is the hardest of the Four Horsemen to prevent. But modifiable risks include avoiding smoking, insulin resistance, obesity, and potential pollution exposure. While cancer treatment options exist, they're less effective than those for cardiovascular disease and metabolic dysfunction. Early detection is key, with aggressive screening being crucial to catch smaller, less mutated tumors for easier treatment. Despite financial, emotional, and incidental risks of screening, the benefits of catching cancer early outweigh these concerns. There's hope for progress through improved screening and treatments like immunotherapy, potentially transforming cancer into a manageable condition.

REFLECTION QUESTIONS FOR CHAPTER EIGHT

Activity: gain insight into your cancer risk

Family History

Does your family have a history of cancer? Make a list of anyone in your family who has died of cancer. At what age were they diagnosed? Could early detection have helped them?

_____

_____

_____

_____

_____

Make a plan for early detection. This can include talking to your doctor about your family history of cancer and scheduling a colon cancer screening at the age of forty.

_____

_____

_____

_____

_____

Think about lifestyle factors that might be contributing to your risk of cancer, including poor diet and smoking. List them here along with your goals on how to improve.

_____

_____

_____

_____

_____

_____

SUMMARY

Dr. Attia introduces us to a patient of his named Stephanie. Stephanie was a healthy forty year old with no serious medical history. Genetic testing revealed that she was a carrier for the gene, a gene associated with Alzheimer's. Stephanie was devastated upon learning this. But Dr. Attia was able to explain to her that, while she had a higher risk of developing Alzheimer's, because she was still relatively young she still had around 25 years to do everything she could to delay/prevent its onset.

Understanding Alzheimer's

Alzheimer's disease dates back to ancient times when "senility" was observed. Dr. Alois Alzheimer first recognized it in 1906, noting brain abnormalities in a patient named Auguste Deter. However, the disease was forgotten until the late 1960s, when British psychiatrists confirmed dementia as a disease rather than normal aging. Plaques and tangles in patients' brains were linked to cognitive impairment, and in the 1980s, amyloid-beta was identified as a potential cause of Alzheimer's due to its presence in plaques. However, despite numerous drug attempts to target amyloid-beta, they have not shown cognitive benefits, partly because they might be administered too late in the disease's progression. Trials testing early administration of anti-amyloid compounds continue to explore potential reversibility.

Can Neurodegenerative disease be prevented?

At first, researchers were hesitant to say that Alzeimher's might be preventable. But three large European studies have shown that certain lifestyle interventions might have a positive impact.

Dementia is hard to prevent and treat because its early stages are often subtle, with symptoms progressing beyond occasional forgetfulness to noticeable memory issues. The clinical stage known as mild cognitive impairment (MCI) is now recognized, but prior to this, there's a preclinical stage (stage I preclinical Alzheimer's) where pathological changes occur without major symptoms. Over forty-six million people in the US may be in this stage. Similar hidden progression occurs in other neurodegenerative diseases, each with distinct early signs such as movement changes in Parkinson's and mood alterations in Lewy body dementia.

This is why Dr. Attia always presents his patients with a battery of complicated and exhaustive testing. This cognitive testing is administered by specialists and is designed to catch the earliest symptoms of dementia.

Cognitive Reserve

The human brain is extremely resourceful and can often compensate for degeneration by switching the pathways that it uses in problem solving. This is why it is important to build up one's cognitive reserve, or the amount of networks and subnetworks in our brain. This reserve is built up through education, experience and the development of complex cognitive skills such as learning a foreign language or musical instrument.

The Prevention Plan

Dr. Attia maintains cautious optimism for patients like Stephanie despite her high genetic risk for Alzheimer's. The concept of Alzheimer's prevention is emerging, and as our understanding of the disease deepens, treatments and interventions can become more advanced. Unlike cancer prevention, where tools are limited, we possess a broader range of methods to prevent Alzheimer's, aided by improved diagnostics for early cognitive decline. For individuals at risk due to genes like APOE e4, addressing metabolic issues, considering dietary changes, and omega-3 supplementation could be beneficial in maintaining brain health.

There is some evidence that the ketogenic diet can help delay cognitive decline and improve symptoms in those with dementia. Dr. Attia stresses the importance of exercise: it is probably the most effective tool that we have to fight dementia. Both endurance and strength training are important when trying to protect against cognitive decline. Other interventions include improving sleep quality and brushing and flossing one's teeth. Interestingly enough, certain oral bacteria have been linked to cognitive decline.

Although Alzheimer's is difficult to treat, Dr. Attia remains optimistic that lifestyle interventions can help in its prevention.

REFLECTION QUESTIONS FOR CHAPTER NINE

Activity: gain insight into your Alzheimer's risk

Family History
Does your family have a history of Alzheimer's? Research your family's history and make note of any instance of Alzheimer's or other neurodegenerative conditions.

_____

_____

_____

_____

_____

Make a plan for early detection. Consider setting up an appointment with a genetic counselor in order to assess your genetic risk, or taking part in routine cognitive testing.

_____

_____

_____

_____

_____

Dr. Attia stresses the importance of "cognitive reserve." What are some ways you can increase your cognitive reserve? Think about complex cognitive activities that you can partake in such as learning a musical instrument or foreign language.

_____

_____

_____

_____

_____

_____

CHAPTER TEN
THINKING TACTICALLY

SUMMARY

Cancer, diabetes, heart disease and Alzheimer's are all diseases of civilization whose prevalence rose dramatically after the Industrial Revolution. Our environments have changed drastically in the last few hundred years, while our genes have remained the same. This mismatch between genes and environment means we must think tactically about our health in order to improve our longevity.

Dr. Attia breaks down the five tactics we have to improve longevity: exercise, nutrition, sleep, emotional health and exogenous molecules (think supplements or drugs like metformin).
Nutrition and exercise protocols can be very complicated. Dr. Attia always asks his patients these three questions when evaluating their metabolic health:
Are they over nourished or undernourished? That is, are they taking in too many or too few calories?
Are they undermuscled or adequately muscled?
Are they metabolically healthy or not?

Answering these simple questions can go a long way in producing a longevity plan. In the following chapters, Dr. Attia breaks down each of the five tactics and provides general counsel on how to implement them in our lives.

Because every patient is so different, Dr. Attia cannot give extremely specific advice, but he can impart the knowledge necessary in order to give the reader a general groundwork for longevity.

REFLECTION QUESTIONS FOR CHAPTER TEN

Think about your relationship to each of the five tactics of longevity. In the space provided rate your current health in relation to each tactic on a scale of 1-10. Think about which tactics you can improve on and start to formulate a plan for the tactics that might be extra challenging for you.

Exercise

_____

_____

_____

_____

Nutrition

_____

_____

_____

_____

Sleep

_____

_____

_____

_____

Emotional Health

_____

_____

_____

_____

Exogenous Molecules

_____

_____

_____

_____

CHAPTER ELEVEN
EXERCISE

SUMMARY

While the data about what kind of exercise to engage in might be confusing, there is a huge amount of evidence that even a small amount of exercise is greatly beneficial. More than any other tactic, it has the power to determine how you will live your life. If you only adopt one tactic from this book it should be exercise. Going from zero minutes to 90 minutes a week of exercise has the power to drop one's risk of dying of all causes by 14 percent.

Cardiorespiratory Fitness

High aerobic fitness and strength are associated with extended lifespan and healthspan, with the benefits often surprising due to their magnitude. Cardiovascular fitness, measured by VO2 max, stands out as a potent indicator of longevity, revealing the body's capacity to utilize oxygen during exercise. As exercise intensity increases, oxygen demand rises, and higher VO2 max signifies greater aerobic capacity, enabling sustained physical activity. This is important because VO2 max is highly correlated with longevity. Someone in the bottom quartile of VO2 max is nearly four times more likely to die than someone in the top quartile! That significant of a difference cannot be understated. The authors of a large JAMA study on VO2 max concluded: "Cardiorespiratory fitness is inversely associated with long-term mortality with no observed upper limit of benefit. Extremely high aerobic fitness was associated with the greatest survival."

The good news is that VO2 max can be improved with training.

Strength

While it might be surprising to some, there is a multitude of evidence that shows muscle strength to be almost as important as cardio fitness when it comes to longevity. When we train our muscles, our bodies produce important molecules like BDNF, an important component of memory and mental health. It also improves our metabolic health as our muscles learn to use energy more efficiently. Aging means an inevitable loss of muscle mass. Low muscle mass in seniors is highly correlated with death. The good news is that by remaining physically active, you can slow down and even stop the muscle atrophy that comes with age.

The Centenarian Decathlon

Exercise is one of the best ways to improve our healthspan, not just our lifespan. But what kind of exercise should we be doing now to improve our future health?

Dr. Attia presents his patients with a list of everyday activities like the following:

- Hike 1.5 miles on a hilly trail.
- Get up off the floor under your own power, using a maximum of one arm for support.
- Pick up a young child from the floor.
- Carry two five-pound bags of groceries for five blocks.
- Lift a twenty-pound suitcase into the overhead compartment of a plane.
- Balance on one leg for thirty seconds, eyes open. (Bonus points: eyes closed, fifteen seconds.)
- Have sex.
- Climb four flights of stairs in three minutes.
- Open a jar.
- Do thirty consecutive jump-rope skips.

If you want to be able to do these activities in your 7th, 8th, and 9th decade of life, then you have to be training with them in mind. We know that our muscle mass and max VO2 will inevitable decline with age. That is why we must train harder now, so that our max is higher than the average person. If you want to be able to carry two five pounds bags of groceries when you are 90, then you need to be training with two twenty pound bags right now. If you want to be able to hike a 1.5 hilly trail when you are eighty, then you need to be able to run that same trail right now. To be more precise, the harder you train now, the more you will be able to participate in life down the road.

In the next chapter, Dr. Attia will break down how to train for this centenarian decathlon.

REFLECTION QUESTIONS FOR CHAPTER ELEVEN

Activity: prepare yourself for the centenarian decathlon

Training with the future in mind
Think of the everyday activities that you will want to participate in as you age. Make a list of ten of them here:

1. _____
2. _____
3. _____
4. _____
5. _____
6. _____
7. _____
8. _____
9. _____
10. _____

What kind of training do you need to engage in now in order to reach these goals?

_____

_____

_____

_____

_____

CHAPTER TWELVE
TRAINING FOR THE DECATHLON

SUMMARY

Aerobic Efficiency: Zone 2

Dr. Attia believes that zone 2 aerobic workouts are one of the best ways to improve longevity. But what does zone 2 mean? Zone 1 is defined as easy activity (think walking on a flat surface) while zone 5 is all out sprinting. Zone 2 is somewhere between easy and moderate. One way to make sure you are in zone 2: try having a conversation. If you can speak in full sentences, but are not interested in having a conversation, then you are probably in zone 2. If you can speak in full sentences, then you are going too hard. If holding a conversation is easy, then you might need to go harder.

Another way of looking at zone 2 is through the lens of lactic acid. When we exercise, our muscles produce lactic acid. This is why we get a burning feeling in our muscles when we exert ourselves. Zone 2 exercise should not be accompanied by a burning feeling because ideally, we are able to use up all the lactic acid that we produce while in this zone. Once you start to "feel the burn" it might be best to ease up.

The benefits of zone two exercise are many. First it helps our bodies become more metabolically flexible. This means that we can switch easily between glucose and fat as an energy source. People with metabolic syndrome have a hard time using fat as an energy source; they mostly rely on glucose. Zone 2 exercise can help reverse that over reliance on glucose. Zone 2 also helps improve mitochondrial function and helps us generate more of them. Lastly, zone 2 exercise helps the body use excess blood glucose, which is damaging to organs.

Dr. Attia recommends that patients get 3 hours of zone 2 exercise per week. That means four 45 minute sessions every week. It is important to choose an activity that matches one's lifestyle. Walking, jogging, riding a stationary bike or swimming are all great ways to get into zone 2.

Maximum Aerobic Output: VO2 Max

Dr. Attia usually introduces VO2 training after about five or six months for patients who are new to exercise. VO2 training is important because VO2 declines as much as 15 percent per decade. This means that if you want to be able to enjoy aerobic exercises like hiking or cycling in your 80's, you must reach a higher than average Vo2 today.

For VO2 training, you should run, jog, or cycle at the maximum pace you can for four minutes. Be sure to pick a pace that you can sustain over the whole four minutes. Then you will jog at an easy pace for four or more minutes (you need to give your body enough time to recover so that you can reach your maximum level on the next go). You should repeat this anywhere from 4-6 times.

VO2 training is uncomfortable, but the good news is that you only need to train like this once a week in order to get a measurable benefit.

Strength

Humans inevitably lose muscle mass as they age, but did you know that you lose muscle strength two to three times as fast as mass, and power two to three times as fast as strength?

This can be scary to hear, especially for those of us who don't already have a strength training regimen. The good news is we can start training right now in order to slow that decline.

Dr. Attia focuses on the following four elements of strength:
• 	Grip strength, how hard you can grip with your hands, which involves everything from your hands to your lats (the large muscles on your back). Almost all actions begin with the grip.
• 	Attention to both concentric and eccentric loading for all movements, meaning when our muscles are shortening (concentric) and when they are lengthening (eccentric). In other words, we need to be able to lift the weight up and put it back down, slowly and with control. Rucking down hills is a great way to work on eccentric strength, because it forces you to put on the "brakes."
• 	Pulling motions, at all angles from overhead to in front of you, which also requires grip strength (e.g., pull-ups and rows).
• 	Hip-hinging movements, such as the deadlift and squat, but also step-ups, hip-thrusters, and countless single-leg variants of exercises that strengthen the legs, glutes, and lower back.

Grip strength is extremely linked to longevity. Some studies even show that grip strength can directly predict how long someone will live. Dr. Attia tests his patients by having them carry a dumbbell or kettle bell in each hand while walking. Eventually, he wants men to be able to carry their body weight (half of their body weight in each hand) for one minute, and women 75 percent of their body weight. This is a difficult goal, and many of his patients don't even attempt this test until they have been training for a year.

Another great grip strength test is the dead hand. A forty year old man should be able to hang for two minutes, a woman for 90 seconds. Again, this is a difficult test that will take most people many months of training.

Dr. Attia highlights the importance of eccentric movement. Often when we train we focus on the curling up of our bicep, or the pulling up of our pull-up. But it is even more important to focus on the "down" phase of our actions. One great way to train eccentric movement is by hiking downhill with a loaded backpack.

For pulling movement, Dr. Attia recommends using a rowing machine. (This is a great machine for VO2 training as well).

Finally, Dr. Attia recommends doing deadlifts and squats in order to engage in hip hinging movement.

Dr. Attia does not go into much detail when describing strength training exercises. He believes that people will learn best from others who know how to do the exercises, rather than from reading about them in a book.

REFLECTION QUESTIONS FOR CHAPTER TWELVE

Think about the main components of exercise proposed by Dr. Attia. For each component, write down your goals. How will you incorporate it into your workout routine? How many minutes will you spend on each component? Try to come up with a realistic plan that fits your schedule.

Aerobic Efficiency: Zone 2

_____

_____

_____

_____

_____

Maximum Aerobic Output: VO2 Max

_____

_____

_____

_____

_____

Strength Training

_____

_____

_____

_____

_____

_____

CHAPTER THIRTEEN
STABILITY

SUMMARY

If staying active is such an important way to increase healthspan, then why do most people stop being active in their later years? Dr. Attia attributes this lack of movement to injury. Injury is often caused by lack of stability. Even acute, sudden injuries like a torn ACL are the result of weakness and instability building up over a long period of time.

The secret to success in the gym is stability: it is better to go slowly and carefully so that you can build a stable and strong foundation. Dr. Attia cautions against diving right into dad hangs and dead lifts without first assessing and building your stability.

Breath

The first component of stability is actually the way you breathe. Breath training focuses on how proper breathing impacts various physical aspects like rib position, spine shape, and body coordination. Breath quality influences movement efficiency and coordination. An exercise to cultivate awareness and diaphragm strength involves lying on the back with legs elevated, inhaling quietly and expanding the rib cage and belly simultaneously. This method supports stable movement and core activation by enhancing intra-abdominal pressure within the abdominal cylinder. DNS emphasizes the abdomen as a cylinder surrounded by muscle walls, enhancing stability and safe movement through breath control.

Feet

Feet are the foundation for almost every movement we make with our bodies. It is important for our feet to remain evenly grounded as we exercise. It is common for patients to pronate their feet inwards or outwards instead of staying grounded. Dr. Attia recommends "toe yoga" to help train our feet and toes. Toe yoga exercises are available at his website: www.peterattiamd.com/outlive/videos.

Spine and Shoulders

Stability training prioritizes safeguarding the spine, particularly given modern lifestyles that often strain its integrity. The spine encompasses the lumbar, thoracic, and cervical parts. "Tech neck" arises from phone-related hunching. Developing proprioceptive awareness and practicing controlled Cat/Cow movements can enhance spine understanding, segmental control, and load distribution. Our focus should be in achieving controlled movement between extreme flexion and extension, enabling safer and more efficient force transmission, minimizing strain on spinal joints and hinges.

In stability training, the shoulders play a crucial role due to their complexity and evolutionary adaptation. The shoulder blades (scapulae) have great mobility, while the shoulder joint itself is controlled by a network of muscles connecting to the scapula and humerus. This setup sacrifices some stability for a wide range of motion, a trade-off made by our ancestors as they evolved to stand upright. However, the shoulder's vulnerability arises from its numerous muscular attachments. A controlled articular rotation exercise (Scapular CARs) helps enhance scapular positioning and control, contributing to overall stability by reestablishing the brain-muscle connection. To do this exercise, stand with your arms at your sides. Raise your shoulder blades then squeeze them back and together. Next drop them down your back before returning them to their starting point. Eventually the "squares" that you make with your shoulder blades should turn into smooth circles. These types of exercises are important for training our brain's awareness and ability to control our muscles.

Grip Strength

Our hands play a crucial role in fitness and daily activities, serving as our interface with the world. Grip strength and the ability to transmit force efficiently through our hands are essential for pushing and pulling movements, connecting the power of the trunk muscles to the rest of the body. However, modern lifestyles have led to weakened finger strength and neglected grip training, increasing the risk of injuries during movements. Developing grip strength involves focusing on finger involvement and initiating upper body movements from the hands. Grip also matters in reactive situations, such as grabbing a leash or railing for stability. These foundational stability exercises, though seemingly simple, require dedicated focus and practice. While trainers can provide guidance and motivation, it's essential to avoid becoming overly dependent on them and to take responsibility for mastering movement patterns through proprioception and self-assessment. Filming workouts and reviewing videos can aid in identifying gaps between perceived and actual movement, aiding progress and skill development.

REFLECTION QUESTIONS FOR CHAPTER THIRTEEN

Think about the main components of stability proposed by Dr. Attia. For each component, write down your goals. How will you incorporate it into your workout routine? Remember to consult www.peterattiamd.com/outlive/videos for more stability exercise demonstrations.

Breath

_____

_____

_____

_____

_____

Feet

_____

_____

_____

_____

_____

Spine and Shoulders

_____

_____

_____

_____

_____

Grip Strength

_____

_____

_____

_____

_____

CHAPTER FOURTEEN
NUTRITION 3.0

SUMMARY

In this chapter, Dr. Attia explains that nutrition is actually a highly complicated and misunderstood component of health. While many people tout the advantages of one diet over another, there is actually very little that scientists know about diet.

What we do know is this: one should not eat too many calories or too few, one should consume sufficient protein, one should consume enough vitamins and minerals ad one should avoid toxins like mercury and lead. Everything else is uncertain.

Dr. Attia explains that most studies that focus on nutritional epidemiology are deeply flawed, or produce inconclusive results. This is because many potential studies would be unethical (we can't ask one group to only eat ice cream while the other eats only vegetables.) And because humans are notoriously difficult subjects, it is very difficult to get people to adhere to a specific diet, even if they are closely monitored.

For these reasons, Dr. Attia does not recommend a one-diet-fits-all approach. In the next chapter he outlines how you can choose a diet that works best for your individual needs.

REFLECTION QUESTIONS FOR CHAPTER FOURTEEN

Why do you think nutrition is such a complicated topic?

_____

_____

_____

_____

_____

Reflect on your own diet history. Have you ever adopted a specific diet for health reasons? Did it help you reach your health goals?

_____

_____

_____

_____

_____

What are the fundamental nutritional goals that we should always keep in mind?

_____

_____

_____

_____

_____

Think about your goals surrounding longevity. Why do you want to live a happier, healthier life?

_____

_____

_____

_____

_____

CHAPTER FIFTEEN
PUTTING NUTRITIONAL BIOCHEMISTRY INTO PRACTICE

SUMMARY

Dr. Attia introduces SAD, or the standard American diet. SAD is full of calorie dense but nutritionally sparse foods that are highly processed. It is our default food environment, and it is not great for longevity.

Most traditional diets, try to distance the dieter from SAD in one of three ways:
1.   Calorie restriction
2.   Dietary restriction
3.   Time restriction

CR: Calorie Restriction

Excessive calorie consumption underpins numerous health issues because surplus energy gets stored in adipose tissue, potentially leading to complications in various organs and systems. Consuming too many calories significantly influences health aspects discussed in this book, contributing to chronic diseases like metabolic disorders, heart disease, cancer, and Alzheimer's. Eating fewer calories has been shown to extend lifespan in animal studies, though debates remain over the exact mechanisms and potential confounding factors.

Calorie counting offers flexibility in food choices but can lead to hunger if poor decisions are made. Studies on caloric restriction for longevity in humans have yielded conflicting results, with primate studies showing mixed outcomes. One study found that rhesus monkeys on a reduced-calorie diet lived longer and healthier lives, while another study showed no significant difference in lifespan between calorically restricted and control monkeys. Differences in diet quality between the studies, particularly sugar content, emerged as a significant factor, suggesting that the quality of the diet may be as important as its quantity for health outcomes.

There are four main takeaways from these studies:
- Avoiding diabetes and related metabolic dysfunction is important to longevity.
- There seems to be a link between calories and cancer. Cancer occurred 50 percent less among the monkeys on the restricted calorie diet.
- You should consider the quality of the food you are eating in addition to the quantity.
- If you are already eating a high quality diet, slightly restricting calories can still be beneficial.

DR: the Nutritional Biochemistry Diet

Dietary restriction (DR) involves excluding certain foods to reduce caloric intake. It can be effective for weight loss, but choosing the right foods to restrict is crucial. While carbohydrate restriction can reduce appetite and choices, fat restriction can backfire if not done correctly. DR's effectiveness varies based on individual metabolism, making personalized approaches essential. Some people might lose a lot of weight on a ketogenic diet, while others might actually gain weight and see their biomarkers go haywire.

There is also still the risk of overnutrition with DR. It is still very possible to consume too many calories even if one is cutting out all sugar, fat, animal products, etc.

Alcohol

Alcohol's unique characteristics make it important to consider as its own macronutrient category. It lacks nutritional value, disrupts fat oxidation, and often leads to mindless eating. While moderate alcohol consumption has been linked to potential cardiovascular benefits, its negative impact on health, such as its carcinogenic nature and associations with Alzheimer's disease, outweigh potential benefits. For mindful enjoyment, limiting alcohol to fewer than seven servings per week and no more than two servings on any given day is recommended by Dr. Attia.

Carbohydrates

Carbs create confusion for many people: are they necessary for good health, or should they be completely eliminated? Dr. Attia says that carbs are neither good nor bad. Research does show, however, that keeping one's blood sugar level stable throughout the day can greatly improve longevity. Because carbs are the nutrient most likely to cause blood sugar swings, one should be careful to not consume them in excess.

Dr. Attia recommends that his patients purchase a Continuous Glucose monitor, or CGM. This device is placed in the arm in such a way that it can provide real time data about one's blood sugar level. Having a CGM for just a few months helps patients understand what foods cause a large and sudden spike in blood sugar. Having access to this data helps them know what foods to eat and which ones to avoid, while also helping them modify their behavior. It is one thing to know that a piece of chocolate cake will spike your blood sugar, it's another to see the consequences of our food choices in real time with a CGM.

After monitoring his own glucose levels closely, Dr. Attia realized that many different variables can affect it. In general, people are more insulin sensitive in the morning. This means late night bingeing is especially bad for spiking glucose. The amount of sleep one gets plays another role in glucose production. More sleep is always better for glucose regulation. Finally, aerobic exercise can help remove excess glucose and regulate blood sugar.

Protein

Protein is the essential building block of our bodies. Dr. Attia recommends that his patients get at least 1.6 g/kg/day of protein, or twice the recommended daily allowance in the US. The ideal amount varies person to person, but for some it might be necessary to increase protein consumption to 2.2 g/kg/day. This is because protein is fundamental in muscle mass production. In order to get 150 grams of protein, Dr. Attia eats a protein shake, a high-protein snack, and two protein meals every day.

Keep in mind that plant protein is not as bioavailable as animal protein, and is missing several key amino acids.

Fats

Carbohydrates provide fuel, amino acids are building blocks, and fats serve both functions efficiently, acting as a fuel source and building blocks for hormones, cell membranes, and brain health. Three main types of fats include saturated fatty acids, monounsaturated fatty acids, and polyunsaturated fatty acids, with distinctions based on their chemical structures. Omega-3 and omega-6 polyunsaturated fatty acids are further subcategories, with marine and nonmarine sources like seafood, nuts, and flaxseed.

Dr. Attia recommends that MUFA's (monounsaturated fats) make up most of the fat in our diet. This usually looks like eating more olive oil and nuts while cutting back on soybean, corn, and sunflower oil.

TR: The Case For And Against Fasting

Fasting is a newly popular diet that has some benefits but also serious drawbacks. While fasting, our insulin levels go down, the liver is emptied of fat, and the body starts burning fat. However, the scientific literature on fasting is weak at best, and human trials have failed to replicate much of the magical weight loss promised by fasting diets. It is also very difficult to consume sufficient protein while engaging in intermittent fasting leading to muscle loss. Subjects who engaged in alternate day fasting also reported much lower activity levels. While some people do lower their blood sugar and lose weight while fasting, the combination of less protein and less exercise might be detrimental to their health.

Dr. Attia does admit that fasting might be a solution for those struggling severely with their metabolic health. For obese patients who have tried and failed to lose fat, he recommends a hypocaloric diet for five days every month. Depending on your weight, a hypocaloric diet can be as little as 700 calories a day for five days straight. While drastic, this measure has been successful in helping Dr. Attia's most overweight patients get back on track metabolically.

REFLECTION QUESTIONS FOR CHAPTER FIFTEEN

What are the three different types of diets? How do they work?

_____

_____

_____

_____

_____

Reflect on your current diet. What percentage of macronutrients are you eating everyday? Are you getting the recommended amount of protein?

_____

_____

_____

_____

_____

Have you ever monitored your blood sugar? What trends did you notice? If you haven't already, consider the benefits of daily blood sugar monitoring.

_____

_____

_____

_____

_____

Think about your goals surrounding nutrition. Brainstorm some ideas to help you reach your fitness and health goals.

_____

_____

_____

_____

_____

CHAPTER SIXTEEN
THE AWAKENING

SUMMARY

Many studies show that chronic insufficient sleep (less than seven hours a night on average) is linked to adverse health outcomes, ranging from susceptibility to sickness to dying from a heart attack. It wreaks havoc on our hormones and can lead to metabolic issues, including type 2 diabetes.

Sleep And Metabolism

Sleep deprivation has a significant impact on metabolism, even in the short term, leading to insulin resistance. Studies consistently show that poor sleep increases insulin resistance by up to a third, a finding supported by both experimental and epidemiological evidence. Long-term observations reveal connections between short sleep duration and increased risks of type 2 diabetes, metabolic syndrome, hypertension, cardiovascular diseases, coronary heart diseases, and obesity. This suggests that inadequate sleep can lead to chronic metabolic dysfunction, potentially causing diseases like NASH, type 2 diabetes, and heart disease.

Sleep and Cardiovascular Disease

The sympathetic nervous system's role in elevating stress hormones and heart rate may explain why poor sleep is closely linked to cardiovascular disease. Chronic poor sleep keeps this system in a perpctual state of alert, leading to elevated blood pressure and heart rate. Long-term insufficient sleep is associated with a higher risk of cardiac events, with studies showing a 6 to 26 percent increase in cardiovascular disease among those with short sleep durations. Genetic research also suggests that adequate sleep can reduce the risk of heart disease, even for individuals with a genetic predisposition. Consequently, prioritizing good sleep is essential for both personal and patient well-being.

Sleep and the Brain

Sleep plays a critical role in both daily cognitive function and long-term cognitive health, particularly as we age. Research shows that poor sleep can potentially cause Alzheimer's disease and dementia, not just be an early symptom. As we enter sleep, various physiological changes occur, including slowed heart rate, reduced core temperature, and regular breathing, all while the brain begins its own processes. Sleep consists of well-defined stages, each serving a specific function and characterized by unique electrical brain wave patterns. Deep non-REM sleep, essential for neurological health, dominates the first half of the night, with brain waves slowing to an extremely low frequency. During a typical night, our sleep cycles between deep non-REM sleep and rapid eye movement (REM) sleep, with each cycle lasting around ninety minutes. In REM sleep, our brains engage in vivid dreaming, and while our electrical brain activity resembles wakefulness, our bodies remain paralyzed to prevent acting out dreams. Both REM and deep non-REM sleep are essential for memory and learning. Deep sleep helps consolidate memories for long-term storage, while REM sleep promotes creativity, problem-solving, and procedural memory. REM sleep also plays a vital role in processing emotional memories, helping separate emotions from memory, and maintaining emotional awareness. Deprivation of REM sleep can hinder emotional understanding and memory processing.

Assessing Your Sleep

Dr. Attia does not recommend relying on sleep medications, as they often trade sleep quantity for quality. One notable exception is trazodone, an anti-depressant that in small doses can actually improve the quality of sleep. Ashwagandha is another sleep aid that might help improve sleep quality. The first step towards improving sleep is acknowledging the need for better sleep quality and duration. Assess your sleep habits using sleep trackers, which estimate sleep metrics like duration and stage with reasonable accuracy. It's also important to evaluate your sleep quality over the last month using validated sleep questionnaires like the Pittsburgh Sleep Quality Index, which covers various aspects of sleep patterns and quality, or the Epworth Sleepiness scale, both of which can easily be found online. Lastly, consider the possibility of obstructive sleep apnea, a common yet underdiagnosed condition. You can use the STOP-BANG questionnaire, which correlates well with formal sleep apnea tests, to assess your risk. If you snore, have high blood pressure, feel consistently tired, or if your partner notices you stop breathing briefly during sleep, consult a medical professional for further testing. Additional risk factors include a BMI over thirty and being male. Sleep apnea can have significant implications for cardiovascular health and dementia risk.

Sleeping Better

To improve your sleep, prioritize creating a dark sleeping environment. Darkness is essential for good sleep, so make your bedroom as dark as possible. Install room-darkening curtains if needed, and remove all sources of light, including electronic devices with bright LEDs. Be cautious of digital clocks, as they can disrupt your sleep if you wake up and see the time. It's important to minimize exposure to artificial light in the evening, as it disrupts your natural circadian rhythm and inhibits melatonin release, the hormone that signals your brain it's time to sleep.

Minimize exposure to blue light, especially from LED household lighting, in the evening as it can interfere with sleep by signaling your brain that it's daytime. Reduce bright LED light exposure before bedtime and consider using warmer LED bulbs. Electronic devices like phones and laptops emit blue light and stimulate your mind, making it harder to sleep. Passive devices like TVs and books are less disruptive to sleep. Avoid screens and social media at least an hour before bedtime, and keep computers and phones out of the bedroom. Maintaining a cooler bedroom temperature, around 65°F, can aid sleep, as your body naturally cools when you fall asleep. A warm bath before bed may help with this process by lowering your core temperature. Cooling mattresses and mattress toppers are also available for those who prefer a cooler sleeping environment.

Alcohol initially acts as a sedative, aiding falling asleep, but it disrupts sleep in the later part of the night, affecting REM sleep and causing more awakenings. Even moderate alcohol consumption can impact memory, cognition, and daytime sleepiness. For middle-aged and older individuals, who may be more sensitive to alcohol's effects, this can be concerning. Limiting alcohol to around two drinks in the evening is advisable for better sleep and next-day performance. Caffeine, found in coffee, works as a sleep blocker by inhibiting the sleep-inducing chemical adenosine. It can disrupt sleep if consumed in excess or at the wrong time. Caffeine tolerance varies among individuals, with some metabolizing it quickly, while others should limit consumption to one or two cups before noon to avoid sleep disturbances.

Cultivating the right amount of sleep pressure at the right times is crucial for healthy sleep. Sleep restriction, limiting the hours of sleep to build up sleep pressure, is a technique to treat insomnia. Napping during the day can reduce sleep pressure and hinder nighttime sleep. Exercise, especially sustained endurance exercise like zone 2, can promote sleep pressure but should be done a few hours before bedtime. Exposure to natural daylight helps regulate the circadian cycle for better sleep. Mentally preparing for sleep involves avoiding stress-inducing activities like checking work emails or the news, as they activate the sympathetic nervous system. Writing down concerns or practicing meditation can help calm the mind and prepare for sleep.

When faced with true insomnia, the first step is to determine if it's genuine insomnia or a mismatch with your natural sleep patterns. If you're lying awake in bed, unable to sleep, it's often better to get up, go to another room, and engage in a relaxing but purposeless activity, such as reading a dull book. Avoid using this time for work or tasks that give insomnia a purpose, as this can reinforce sleeplessness. Additionally, consider that you might be a night owl chronotype, and adjusting your bedtime accordingly could be helpful.

If insomnia persists despite these efforts, Cognitive Behavioral Therapy for Insomnia (CBT-I) is an effective treatment. CBT-I aims to restore confidence in one's ability to sleep by breaking bad sleep habits and addressing any underlying anxieties about sleep. Sleep restriction is a technique used in CBT-I to increase sleep pressure, ultimately improving sleep quality and confidence. Research indicates that CBT-I is more effective than sleeping medications for treating insomnia.

REFLECTION QUESTIONS FOR CHAPTER SIXTEEN

Why is sleep so important for longevity?

_____

_____

_____

_____

_____

Assess your current sleep schedule. How many hours of good sleep do you get on average? Rate the quality and quantity here:

_____

_____

_____

_____

_____

How does sleep quantity and quality effect our metabolism?

_____

_____

_____

_____

_____

Think about how you can improve your sleep. Using the ideas from this chapter, create an outline for your optimal bedtime routine here:

_____

_____

_____

_____

_____

CHAPTER SEVENTEEN
WORK IN PROGRESS

SUMMARY

Mental health is one of the most important components of longevity. In this chapter, Dr. Attia dives into the abuse he experienced as a child, and how he was forced to confront it while at a patient at the Bridge, a clinic for mental health.

The Trauma Tree framework used at the Bridge provides insight into how undesirable adult behaviors, like addiction and uncontrolled anger, can stem from childhood trauma adaptations. Trauma is categorized into five main types: abuse (physical, sexual, emotional, or spiritual), neglect, abandonment, enmeshment (blurred boundaries between adults and children), and witnessing tragic events. These traumas can be either "big-T" traumas, like rape, or "little-t" traumas, such as having an alcoholic parent. Both types can significantly impact a person's life, but little-t trauma can be more challenging to address, often because it's dismissed. In essence, trauma, whether big T or little t, is defined by moments of perceived helplessness, which may not always be life-or-death but can profoundly affect a child's developing brain.

Childhood trauma's impact lies in how a child adapts to it, and while children can be remarkably resilient, these adaptations can lead to maladaptive and dysfunctional adult behaviors. The four branches of the trauma tree illustrate this dysfunction: addiction, codependency, habituated survival strategies (like anger), and attachment disorders. Identifying these branches can be relatively straightforward, but addressing the roots is the challenging part, as responses to trauma are highly individual. There's no quick fix or pill to erase trauma or its adaptations; it requires hard work and often a lengthy process of healing.

Addressing emotional health is a unique challenge, as it doesn't fit neatly into the disease-based model that Medicine 2.0 often uses. Emotional health is distinct from mental health, encompassing how we regulate emotions and manage relationships. While clinical mental illnesses have recognizable symptoms, emotional health issues are broader and less easily categorized. Medicine 2.0 struggles to address these complexities.

A paradigm shift, similar to the one from Medicine 2.0 to Medicine 3.0, is needed to approach emotional health proactively, much like preventing cardiovascular disease. Recognizing potential issues early and committing to long-term solutions tailored to each individual is key. This approach aims to prevent clinical mental health conditions like depression and anxiety.

Addressing emotional health requires ongoing effort and daily practice, akin to maintaining physical health through exercise or nutrition. The challenge is that many individuals may not recognize the need for change, unlike the clear signs of physical health problems. Proactivity in managing emotional health can lead to a better overall healthspan, especially in later life.

After decades of depression, anger and relationship issues. Dr. Attia found help with a system called dialectical behavior therapy (DBT), a psychology approach developed by Marsha Linehan. DBT, rooted in cognitive behavioral therapy principles, helps individuals with severe emotional issues, even those with borderline personality disorder. DBT is evidence-based and skills-focused, involving daily workbook exercises with a therapist. It centers around five pillars: mindfulness, emotional regulation, distress tolerance, interpersonal effectiveness, and self-management. Dr. Attia particularly focuses on emotion regulation and distress tolerance, striving to widen his "distress tolerance window" by prioritizing factors like exercise, sleep, and self-care in order to minimize emotional outbursts.

DBT relies on mindfulness, a tool to create space between stimulus and response. Mindfulness meditation has helped Dr. Attia detach from his thoughts and emotions, providing flashes of insight. It's about creating a gap to avoid reflexive reactions, allowing for calmer, more rational responses to situations. Mindfulness also highlights that suffering often stems from thoughts about past or future events, not immediate causes. Dr. Attia learned to listen to his self-talk and reframe it by treating himself as he would a friend, shifting from self-judgment to self-kindness. Recording voice memos and sending them to his therapist helped transform his harsh inner dialogue into a more forgiving and wise one.

DBT aims to help individuals regulate their emotions and manage distress. Dr. Attia struggled with anger rooted in shame, leading to a cycle of shame and anger. DBT teaches techniques for distress tolerance, emotion recognition, and coping. Dr. Attia uses sensory interventions like ice water or cold showers to stimulate the vagus nerve and shift to a calmer state. Slow, deep breathing is another helpful tool. DBT requires conscious thought and action, including "opposite action" to change underlying emotions. Dr. Attia shares an example of practicing opposite action by spending quality time with his family despite work stress, resulting in a positive change in mood.

Dr. Attia firmly believes that everyone can make changes to their lives to improve their mental and emotional health. While difficult, these changes are worthwhile: they help us to live longer, and give us the desire to increase our healthspan.

REFLECTION QUESTIONS FOR CHAPTER SEVENTEEN

What are the five main types of trauma?

_____

_____

_____

_____

_____

How is emotional health different from mental health?

_____

_____

_____

_____

_____

What is DBT and how does it help people heal?

_____

_____

_____

_____

_____

Think about your own mental and emotional health. If you are struggling, what are some steps you might take to begin or continue your healing journey?

_____

_____

_____

_____

_____

Made in the USA
Las Vegas, NV
12 March 2024

87084144R00035